The Unvoiced Pain

Releasing Depression and Anxiety

Danielle M. Gilbert
Visionary Author

Co-Authored By:
Destini Braxton, Dr. Shantell Chambliss, Stacy Crawley, Joi Donaldson, Dr. Shonda Harris-Muhammed, Andrea "Aj" Sanders, Dr. Tabatha Spurlock, Tiffany Winfield

Copyright © 2022 by Danielle M. Gilbert
All Rights Reserved. This book, nor any portion thereof, may not be reproduced or used in any manner whatsoever without the expressed written permission of the publisher except for the use of brief quotations in a book review.

Printed in the United States of America.

ISBN: 979-8-218-05157-0
Edited, Formatted and Published by Empower Her Publishing, LLC

Table of Contents

Introduction v

Foreword by *Danielle M. Gilbert*........................... vii

Motherhood Metamorphosis by *Destini Braxton*..... 1

Hannah's Hope by *Dr. Shantell Chambliss*............. 9

Reclaiming My Power by *Stacy Crawley*............... 19

Healing Beyond the Veil by *Joi Donaldson*............ 27

I Fought My Way Back
by *Dr. Shonda Harris-Muhammed*........................ 33

BODIES In BOXES
by *Andrea "Aj" Sanders*..................................... 41

No More Running
by *Dr. Tabatha M.W. Spurlock*............................ 51

The Power of Vulnerability
by *Tiffany Winfield*... 59

Conclusion... 67

Introduction

Unexplainable sadness. Lack of fulfillment. Self-doubt. Worry. Fear. Procrastination. Unproductivity. Extreme productivity. Loneliness…in a world surrounded by people who love you.

These are typical emotions of someone suffering from depression. Depression is a mental illness that overtakes the thoughts and feelings of a person. It usually develops from stressful or traumatic events, family history, after giving birth, suffering from an illness, excessive drug and alcohol use or through personality traits like low self-esteem or lack of self-confidence. Despite the misconception, depression is not something that one develops intentionally or just gets over. It very much plagues an individual, disrupting their normal and healthy way of life. In many instances, depression unfortunately also leads to anxiety.

In this book, nine women courageously share their truths about their struggles with depression and anxiety. These women are wives, business owners, mothers and mentors. They're highly ambitious role models in their communities, their churches, and their homes. Yet, they were not off limits to the disease that attacks millions of people across the globe. Their greatest hope for you is that you realize that it's okay to acknowledge you're suffering. That acknowledgement is the first step towards your healing. Next, it's okay to seek help. Help is available in various modalities based upon your needs and comfort level. Do what feels right for you. It's time to release depression and anxiety. It's time to release the unvoiced pain.

Foreword
Danielle M. Gilbert

According to the Anxiety and Depression Association of America, anxiety disorders:

- are the most common mental illnesses in the U.S.
- affect 40 million adults in the United States aged 18 and older.
- comprise 18.1% of the population every year.

Although the disorders are treatable, only 36.9% of those suffering seek treatment. Three out of five people suffering from anxiety and depression are more likely to go to the doctor and are six times more likely to be hospitalized.

Depression is a widespread mental health disorder affecting people from all walks of life. Its many symptoms can impede a person's ability to function normally in social settings, work, or school. Millions of adults will experience depression at some point in their lives and at least 50% of people dealing with depression also have an anxiety disorder.

In 1998, I was one of the millions of adults who suffered from depression and anxiety. At a young age, I lost my mother to leukemia. The pain from loss continued through the next six months with the deaths of important family members. My uncle passed, then my aunt died from cancer. Soon after, another aunt was set on fire by her husband and then my grandfather died from old age. I often asked, "Why me? God, why are you taking the people I love from me?" I never thought the deaths would end. Every other month another precious soul left to enter the gates of heaven. Eventually, I lost another aunt, two uncles, grandfather, and cousin.

Losing my firstborn at six months old due to shaken baby syndrome by his father, plus hiding from the world as a teenage mother created another layer of pain. The feeling of emptiness led to increased depression, which led to anxiety about not feeling loved or good enough. During my early 20s, I felt immobilization anxiety. Because anxiety often leads to depression, it was so bad for me that I couldn't even leave the house sometimes. I didn't want to think about going to work or anywhere else. Kneeling and crying became my daily routine. When I wasn't kneeling, I was lying in bed, looking at the sky still asking, "Why? Why me, Lord? What did I do for You to take my loved ones away?" Then I'd ask Him to please help me progress through the steps of grief. I wanted to heal from the emotions of confusion.

Slowly, I felt better...but not for long. I took one step forward to only take two steps backward. The signs of progress were challenging to realize. Daily, I found a poem or quote to guide me through the pain of death. I needed help! The following year, progress started with the realization of being in touch with the finality of the deaths. I finally knew my loved ones were not returning; however, they had entered the gates of eternal life. They

Foreword

will never return to earth, but their memories must remain alive. The pleasant and unpleasant memories run through my mind day after day. Reminiscing on the memories became painful and I looked to my family and friends to share the happy memories of our loved ones. Getting out of bed no longer became a daunting task. It was the best sensation when I could drive to my destination without crying the entire time, look forward to the holidays, sit through a church service without crying, or even have patience with myself through "grief attacks." I knew they were becoming further apart and less frightening and painful.

Whew, patience. I never understood how to be patient with life - most notably, God's plan for me. Through the pain of death, learning myself, and praying, I never knew God was preparing me for His destiny. Or rather, my destiny that He designed especially for me. Some days it was a lot harder to be patient. Day after day, I prayed with no response. I wondered why my prayers were falling on deaf ears. Why wouldn't God move me into a place of happiness? Sitting on the edge of my bed on a Sunday afternoon, I prayed to the Spirit to fill, empower, and direct me as I waited on the Lord. The silence was slowly killing me inside. I felt Him wrap His arms around me and it allowed me to take the leap of faith and courage to start multiple businesses.

In 2013, the mask was removed, the fear was erased, the pain was eased, and the decision to be the authentically M.E. happened within months. Unfortunately, a setback occurred while working in corporate America. I found my spirits fighting against demons, fighting to prove I was a leader, fighting to climb the corporate ladder while others around me gained opportunities that were not afforded to me, all while trying to be the Authentic ME! In 2018, the fight was over. I fired "My BOSS" and became "The BOSS." I vowed to never go back for another job where my voice was not valued, my values were not aligned with the company's values, or a mask had to be worn to fit in. So, the race to win started quickly.

I have overcome my battle with anxiety and depression, the desire to be loved, and the feeling that I am not good enough through writing daily affirmations and gratitude statements. The acknowledgment that I was suffering from anxiety and depression helped me begin practicing self-care and meditation. In addition to practicing self-care, I found 12 practical actions to guide me when getting out of bed seems impossible.

The following 12 action-oriented practices come from mindfulness-centered cognitive-behavioral therapy (CBT), the best-tested approach to managing anxiety and depression. Choose one to practice each day for the best results; consistency is key. Note: These practices are adapted from The CBT Deck for Anxiety, Rumination, and Worry.

Practical Actions:

1. Set Your Sights

Anxiety and depression often fill our minds with potential problems and feared failures as though we're victims of circumstance. Start to turn the tables. Decide

Foreword

first thing in the morning what kind of day you will have. What thoughts will you cultivate? How will you find joy? Who will you love? What quality of presence will you bring to any challenges you meet? You are the author of your days. Decide what is worthy of your energy and attention.

2. Worry vs. Problem Solving

Worrying is repetitive and unproductive, but it can often feel like you're working through problems. Authentic problem solving, in contrast, is a focused way of finding solutions. When you're worrying today, figure out whether there's an actual problem to solve or if your mind is simply spinning its wheels. Then aim to redirect your mental energy toward productive problem-solving.

3. Find Strength

When you find yourself hoping for an easy, problem-free day, shift your focus to how you'll respond. Say to yourself, "May I find strength to meet every challenge. May I find the courage to face whatever comes my way. May I find grace in all I do." Problems are inevitable. How you handle them is up to you.

4. Define Your Best Life

When you're tempted to avoid something today because of anxiety, ask yourself what kind of life you want to have lived. One defined by fear and avoidance? One where you played it safe, even when it meant missing out on things you cared about? Or a life of defying fear and inertia to do what mattered to you? Plan to take one action today that your future self will thank you for.

5. Take the Wheel

Emotions are noisy passengers directing you to avoid anything that makes you anxious or seems overwhelming. Careful! Don't go there! Watch out! Consider today whether you want avoiding complicated feelings to be the top priority in your life. Is there something more important to you than being emotionally comfortable? If so, steer your life in that direction and let your feelings come along for the ride.

6. Love Conquers Fear

Love and fear are opposing forces—as one grows, the other shrinks. When you're feeling anxious or down today, ask yourself, "How can I show love to someone else?" Look for opportunities to meet the needs of those around you, even in ways they aren't expecting. Focus on the act of loving rather than waiting to feel loved and see what happens. Let love be the antidote to fear.

7. Change the Conversation

Anxiety and depression often make themselves the center of our attention, leading us to ask questions like: "Why do I feel so depressed? How can I stop feeling anxious?" When you're struggling emotionally today, ask a different question: "What task needs my attention right now?" Then redirect your energy toward doing what needs to be done, allowing your feelings to exist in the background.

8. Face Your Fears

Avoiding the things that make you uncomfortable strengthens your fears and makes your world smaller. The best way to reduce unrealistic fears is to gradually face them. Pay attention today for signs of avoidance, like putting off a task you're unsure how to do or taking a longer route when driving because it bypasses roads that make you nervous. Pick one action you can take today to move courageously through fearful avoidance.

9. Move Through Procrastination

Falling behind on your to-do list can lead to stress, anxiety, and feeling overwhelmed. Pick something you've been putting off and commit to doing the first small step of it today. For example, gather up all the dirty clothes if you need to do laundry. Getting started boosts mood, lowers anxiety and makes it easier to keep working on the task.

10. Maximize Outdoor Time

Being in nature is known to lower anxiety and boost mood. Set a goal to be outside as much as possible today. Find any excuse to step outdoors, even for a few seconds. Go for a short walk. Open the mail outside. Dine al fresco. Take in your surroundings — the sky, the light, the plants, and the birds. Feel your spirit connect with the natural world. Please focus on the experience itself rather than on whether it's helping you feel better.

11. Practice Kindness

Caring for others effectively redirects our attention away from our preoccupation with how we feel. When you're stuck under challenging emotions today, think of something excellent you could do for someone you know, whether a loved one or an acquaintance. What would brighten their day? Allow anxious or depressed moods to be a trigger for acts of kindness, however unexpected or even undeserved.

12. Can I be Open to This?

Difficult emotions often push us to resist reality — to close ourselves off and say no to what's happening. When you're confronted with something difficult today, ask yourself, "Can I open up to this? Am I willing to stay with my experience?" Greater peace is available when we summon the courage to face life just as it is.

When your life appears to have stopped, and everything seems unbearable, remember you are in control. There isn't a rapid cure for anxiety or depression and having health anxiety is a natural part of the human experience. However, it is a problem when your anxiety is interfering with daily living. Learning to recognize your symptoms, as well as your triggers, and working to manage them is an excellent first step. I know from personal experience. You have this, so go out in the world to #begreat!

Motherhood Metamorphosis
Destini Braxton

"One, two, three... PUSH!" Ten minutes passed. "Push!" Thirty minutes passed. "Push." fifty minutes passed. "PUSH. This is it." Wow, an hour of pushing and I finally heard my baby boy cry. On October 3, 2019, I gave birth to my first child, and a new me, at that very moment. I was now a first-time mother holding my son in my arms. My healthy 7 pounds and 15-ounce baby who I named Elijah Christian Edwards. This was truly the happiest day of my entire life. Everybody helped prepare me for this moment, but what they didn't help me prepare for mentally or physically was the postpartum stage of life.

My days grew longer and lonely after coming home from the hospital with Elijah. I did not want to answer people's phone calls or texts, but I wanted people to contact me. I was depressed and didn't know it. My twin sister noticed it before I did and that's when I decided to speak up at my postpartum check-up. I had to answer a questionnaire composed of questions that asked...

Do you cry for no reason?

Do you think of harming yourself?

Do you blame yourself for things out of your control?

Have you found less joy in activities that once brought you joy?

Once I realized that I was circling "always" or "almost always", I immediately felt ashamed. My doctor told me that I was experiencing postpartum depression and anxiety and not just the baby blues.

I experienced a lot of anxiety and began to live my motherhood days out of fear. I was afraid to drive with Elijah in the car because I thought I was going to get in a car accident, at no fault of my own, every time I drove somewhere. It would take me at least fifteen minutes of redirecting my thoughts and constant repetition of "God is watching over you and your baby. You can do this." I wouldn't hold my son and walk around with him because I thought I might accidentally drop him, no matter how careful I was trying to be. I was afraid of giving him a bath because I had a fear of him drowning in the bathtub even though I would hold him tight. It was the thoughts that were in control of my life instead of allowing God to be in control. I had days where I couldn't get out of bed, but did because my son couldn't take care of himself.

I thought about suicide on my first Mother's Day because I felt like a failure as a mother. Elijah's father moved out and I was too depressed to be the perfect mother - let alone define what a perfect mother looked like. What stopped me?! Oh, I remember I tried to write a letter to my son and niece about my decision. I couldn't write it because it made me extremely heartbroken and sad knowing that my son and niece would never get to do "kiss attacks", make memories, or feel my love in person. I felt as if they were the only two that loved me and wanted me around no matter how imperfect I was. I didn't want to be the first person they had to say goodbye to. Why did I keep thinking of suicide as the solution? Honest answer: I didn't really want to. I just wanted the pain to go away. I was tired of feeling alone, mentally and physically. I was tired of being seen as a burden to Elijah's father because I couldn't do my part for the household. All I did was blame myself for everything that went wrong in my life after having a child. Simple things that weren't actually my fault, yet I carried the blame. I would cry every time I changed Elijah's diaper and he had a diaper rash because I kept thinking, "If only I could've changed his diaper sooner, then he wouldn't have a rash." I cried every time my family tried to give me suggestions and parenting advice because I perceived it as them not believing in me as a mother or that they knew my child better than I did. "Well, you need to stop that," I told myself. "You have a son to raise and he needs his mommy." I wanted help but didn't know how to ask for it or what I wanted it to look like. I just wanted to be enough for Elijah and for myself.

In 2021, I became pregnant again. Showing up to my 8-week ultrasound appointment and seeing that I was having twins was the best feeling ever. I wasn't just carrying one blessing, but two!!! In the blink of an eye, I experienced joy and sorrow. Only one of my twins had a heartbeat and I will never be able to let go of that image or moment. I hid my emotions until I got to the car, but the tears wouldn't stop flowing. I sent texts to my loved ones because I didn't want to share my pain. This was a tough one to sit with! I was a twin having twins, but would only be welcoming and embracing one. That was hard for me to process. I blamed myself for what happened, even though I did everything right. "How could this happen to me?! What did I do to deserve this?!" I did nothing wrong and I needed to reshape my focus around the situation. I will always hold April 26, 2021 close to my heart because I gained an angel that day. Even though I don't get to hold that baby in my arms, love on my baby, or watch my baby grow up with his or her brothers, I will always remind myself that he or she is looking down amazed at how wonderful his or her mommy is today.

There were plenty of days when I didn't think I would even see my son turn one or two years old. But guess what?! I did. I even celebrated Elijah's birthday while carrying his little brother! I welcomed my second son into this world with so much love and happiness on November 29, 2021. This was another amazing day and I could not believe that I was finally holding my second son. An official super boy mom! When I held him for the first time, the sadness immediately crept in because I should have been welcoming and holding two healthy babies. I was still overjoyed at how precious and blessed my 5 pounds and 13-ounce baby turned out to be.

God is within her, she will not fail.
Psalms 46:5

Motherhood Metamorphosis

I wish I knew then that my dark, depressing, and anxious days would eventually become better controlled. My kids need me, but most importantly, I need me. I am in a much better and stronger mental place, in which I am glad to share my testimony! It was an uphill journey that depended on journaling, weekly therapy, mental breaks, deep and authentic conversations, and self-reflection. I began to speak up and share my experience with postpartum depression and anxiety because I knew there were other mothers who had experienced what I went through and needed to know they weren't alone. One of the many amazing strategies that I had in place after my second pregnancy was a postpartum mental checklist and a postpartum code with my best friend. The code was important to me because I would find it easier to send a purple heart emoji instead of saying "I'm having intrusive thoughts. Please tell me I am not crazy." Or I would send a black heart emoji in place of saying "I can't do this today. Please come when you can."

Elijah means *Jehovah is my God* and Christian means *follower of Christ*. Judah means *praise* and Gabriel means *God is my strength*. My kids have powerful and purposeful names - each given to them with the intention of them being able to live up to their names. Their names were chosen because they were given to me during a time when I needed to rely on my faith to help guide me, heal me, and flourish into who I was created to be. My journey as a mother has not met its final destination yet.

I turned to writing poetry in my notebook because I needed to freely express how I was feeling, without being called crazy. As a conclusion for this chapter, I wanted to

Destini Braxton

share a personal favorite that sheds light on my experience with and healing from postpartum depression and anxiety.

I cried in the shower
But you never knew
Most days I kept asking
How will I push through

Rain on my parade or water me so I can grow.
This motherhood transition feels like a tough blow.
But I will get up and fight this mental battle.
As it begins to rain on random days,
I will continue to reign every day
Speak up
Stay quiet
Does it matter?
Will they understand
No, but so what
They don't matter, you do
Stand up
Be loud
You're not in this alone
Yell "Postpartum depression is real" in the microphone

Do I sleep when you sleep?
Do I clean while you sleep?
Do I do my homework and study while you sleep?
Do I cook before daddy comes home?
Do I eat and take a shower alone while you sleep?
Do I pray to God for happiness and strength while you sleep?

Motherhood Metamorphosis

I just need time
For me
For me to be a better mommy
For me to overcome the postpartum depression and anxiety

I've experienced the storm
Soon I'll see the sunshine
I can't wait to watch my life transform
with my son, I'll be fine

Destini Braxton is a Special Education teacher. She is a strong advocate for special education students and individuals. She is currently working on her Doctorate in Educational Psychology with a research interest in teacher-student relationships, student motivation, trust, and student emotions and mental health.

As a mother of two handsome sons, she is not a stranger to Postpartum Depression and Anxiety. She has experienced negative self-image, low self-esteem, intrusive thoughts, and self-doubt. Fortunately, that has not stopped her from pursuing her dreams, overcoming all obstacles, and recognizing that her journey is not over and her purpose has not been fulfilled.

Destini does an amazing job at sharing her testimony with others and bravely speaks out on the importance of maternal mental health pre and postpartum. She has shared and provided practical and spiritual tips and strategies for overcoming Postpartum Depression and Anxiety and finding one's self postpartum.

Hannah's Hope
Dr. Shantell Chambliss

I Samuel 1:10: "And she was in bitterness of soul, and prayed to the Lord and wept in anguish."

Can you imagine Hannah's frustration in the scripture above? She has a devoted husband who loves her despite her inability to conceive but is being constantly belittled and teased by Peninnah for that very reason. Years have passed, yet she has not given Elkanah the son that she so desperately wants. At this point in her journey, I can imagine that she is at the end of her rope…she isn't getting any younger, her peers are on their second or third child, and her husband has given up hope that she will bear him a child.

You rarely think of infertility as a mental health condition but it is definitely a catalyst. Studies have shown that infertile couples experience significant anxiety and emotional distress.
A diagnosis of infertility can be emotionally and physically challenging leading to depression and isolation.

I personally have experienced both in droves.

A diagnosis of infertility can feel like a death sentence. In many ways, it is. It is the killer of dreams, hopes, and fantasies. The very words scream defeat. In the minutes, seconds, hours, days, weeks, months, and years following that diagnosis you may find yourself feeling alone and isolated as if you are the only woman in the world to learn that having a baby won't be as easy as you once thought.

Trying to conceive is a lonely place...especially when your conception methods don't involve menstrual cycles, ovulation, and sex. Even still, it's very rare to find several people in your circle who are actively trying to conceive and even more rare to find friends who are going through fertility treatments at the same time as you. Eventually, you find yourself in a place and space where having simple conversations with lifelong friends or going to happy hour are almost unthinkable.

If Hannah had lived in today's society, I'm sure she would have been diagnosed with depression, anxiety, and maybe even post-traumatic stress disorder - just like me.

My Story

I struggled with the horrible symptoms of Polycystic Ovary Syndrome (PCOS) for most of my teenage and young adult years. In my early teens, I saw every fertility specialist, holistic healer, and baby expert within a 100-mile radius of my home. I came up with plans to lose weight, cure my fertility issues, and get my house (physical, mental, financial, and spiritual) in order to have a baby. Every single time I started a "baby making regimen" I slacked off and eventually abandoned ship out of sheer frustration. Little did I know, this is where the first signs of my debilitating depression began.

In early 2015, I resolved that THIS was the year that I would fight the infertility monster and that I wouldn't stop until I was barefoot, pregnant, and eating pickles and ice cream for breakfast! I hired a personal trainer, made (another) appointment with the top reproductive endocrinologist in my area, and began eating clean. By July nothing (and I mean nothing) had happened. My fertility issues hadn't subsided and I wasn't any closer to being pregnant. Finally, my reproductive endocrinologist suggested what I had been trying so hard to avoid…in vitro fertilization.

For two months, my husband and I mulled it over, tried to figure out how we would come up with the 5-figure price tag, read our insurance policies backwards and forwards, and finally agreed that it was go time. We claimed October as our start date and it was on and popping. Do people still say that??? Our first in vitro appointment consisted of a baseline ultrasound of my uterus. That ultrasound revealed several uterine polyps that basically shut down our in vitro plans for the time being.

insert sad face here

Fast forward to December…I had surgery to remove the polyps and after three weeks of recovery the in vitro plans were back on.

woot woot

Fast forward again to late February...after WEEKS of hormone pills, injections, suppositories (TMI, I know), egg harvesting, sperm testing, embryo transfers, and bed rest...you guessed it...WE GOT PREGNANT!!! I couldn't believe it. I'd done it! I hadn't given up! I conquered the infertility monster!

insert happy dance here

I immediately went into mommy mode...planning, nurturing, growing, and glowing. Five months in and I was officially a professional mommy. Nursery plans were underway, baby shower date set, and shopping for little Jayden was becoming a daily event.

Everything was perfect...until my cervix opened 19 weeks too early.

After losing my son in 2016, trying to conceive again evolved into a season of extreme isolation. My social and physical activities were limited when I was in an active cycle. The usual fun things were virtually nonexistent: cocktails, having coffee, and.... yes, even sex is off the table at some point during an IVF cycle. My cycles usually lasted three to four weeks (cycles vary by woman) so if we total my eight failed cycles over three years, we're talking 32 weeks of extremely limited socializing. When I crunched the numbers, I began to understand why the invitations stopped coming, my phone rarely rang, and I spent most Friday nights with

Blanche, Rose, Dorothy, and Sophia (we'll discuss my Golden Girls obsession another time).

Remember talking to your best friend on the phone for hours at a time? In this season, avoiding awkward conversations with my friends became an Olympic sport [*insert exasperated sigh here*]. So much so that I grew to a point where I stopped disclosing that we were trying to have a baby because the responses I got became so repetitious that I began to finish the other person's sentence:

> *Me: We're trying to have a baby.*
> *Them: Just have sex every other day.*
> *Them: My friend took some vitamins; you should try those.*
> *Them: Stop thinking about it, it will happen.*
> *Them: Let go and let God.*
> *Them: I got pregnant without even trying. What's wrong with you? (Yes, I've actually heard this several times!)*
> *Them: Lay upside down after you have sex. (Who does this???)*
> *Me: Nevermind.*

If I wasn't dodging unsolicited advice, I was riddled with the guilt of bombarding my friends with stories of daily ultrasounds, shots, pills, hormone rage, and baby anxiety. It really was a proverbial Catch 22. Inevitably, communication with anyone outside of your doctor and your partner becomes a daunting task.

The Reality Check

Women going through fertility treatments need their tribes more than ever - especially black women. A 2017 study revealed that young Black women from middle-class backgrounds feel "different" or even isolated when it comes to Black sisterhood. Couple that with the stigma of infertility and we have a public health crisis bubbling under the surface. In full transparency, in many ways I shut my friends out and, in many ways, they abandoned me.

How did I fix this?

I Prayed But Took Purposeful Action

A good friend reminded me that I am, in fact, a part of a tribe of biblical women who were branded as infertile, overcame unthinkable obstacles, faced unjust ridicule, and ultimately survived their barren season. They were more than conquerors...and so am I. Moreover, the women labeled as "barren" and "crazy" in the Bible are the unequivocal matriarchs of the ancient world. Ironic, isn't it?

Throughout this journey I have leaned heavily on the Word of God. My journals are full of pleas, tears, questions, and concerns. In those notes, I found an overwhelming sense of comfort. The stories of Sarah, Rebekah, Rachel, and of course, Hannah wrapped my broken spirit like a blanket and provided me the strength to press forward.

Hannah's Hope

The beauty of *1 Samuel 1:10* is the transparency in which Hannah is praying to the Lord...in bitterness and anguish. Translation: homegirl is fed up and pissed off! Many of us have been taught that being bitter or angry is wrong but God wants our true heart. He doesn't want you to pretend that everything is ok when it isn't. He wants you to cry out to Him from the depths of your soul. If you're angry, He wants to know. If you're bitter, He wants to know that too! Hannah understood that prayer is a two-way communication with God. She talked to Him and told Him her struggles. Use this time to tell Him your struggles. Tell Him what angers you, what you don't understand, and what has hardened your heart. Pour your soul out before the Lord.

While modern medicine has produced miracles for millions of women, the main remedy for barrenness in the Bible was prayer and divine intercession. I believe that together (biology + bible), anything is possible!
I know we get tired of hearing pray about it so here are a few other tools I used to release the depression associated with my infertility diagnosis:

> **Host a girls' night in.** Bring the party to you. Order everyone's favorite food, make some mocktails, and Netflix and chill. Only rule: NO baby talk!
>
> **Take time off between cycles.** When a cycle fails, it can be a miserable, heartbreaking experience. Give yourself grace...and a few weeks off. During my last two cycles I refused to go right back to shots and pills immediately after the negative

pregnancy test. On those cycle breaks, hubby and I took a mini vacay, I enjoyed the gym, had a few drinks, and had LOTS of sex.

Accept the damn invite! I found myself turning down invites to happy hour, jazz concerts, and cookouts even when I wasn't in an active cycle because I was either coming out of a failed cycle or laser focused on starting the next. If you're in an active cycle maybe skip happy hour but enjoy the concert.

Find your tribe. Conceiving your baby may take weeks, months, or years. Your primary group of girlfriends will need to stretch and grow to accommodate this season of your life. There are several amazing communities for women who are experiencing infertility and/or trying to conceive. I intentionally stepped outside of my comfort zone and found new tribes to supplement my season.

Trying to conceive is a lonely, soul-crushing place. But you don't have to stay there sis. Don't punish yourself for chasing your purpose. Revive your social life and surround yourself in love during this season. Recognize that the wilderness is the space between promise and fulfillment. It's not a fun place but it is a fundamental place. This is where our faith is put to the ultimate test. This is not a time to get angry but a time to rely fully on God. In the wilderness, friends will be scarce (or completely nonexistent), comfort will be unreachable, and having faith will seem like an impossible feat. God tends to send us to the wilderness when He wants our attention. Give it to Him!

Lastly, I challenge you to dream a little. Imagine a healthy, happy future. Dreams revive hope. Write your biggest, boldest dream down and keep it close to your heart and mind.

Shantell J. Chambliss, PhD is an award-winning entrepreneur, business strategist, advocate and philanthropist. As an entrepreneur, Shantell has developed an impressive business portfolio that includes ventures in healthcare, the nonprofit sector, consulting, retail, and cultural arts. A true student of organizational development, Shantell has matched extensive education and training with over 18 years of experience as a coach and consultant to create methods that help businesses launch, grow, and maximize their profit.

Shantell is the CEO and Principal Consultant of **Nonprofitability***, a boutique consulting firm that specializes* in equipping nonprofits and faith-based organizations with proven tools and practices that promote sustainability.

Always keeping community engagement and outreach at the forefront of her work, Shantell founded **Dress for Success® Central Virginia,** a Richmond, VA based affiliate of the international nonprofit organization that empowers women to achieve economic independence by providing a network of support, professional attire and the development tools to help women thrive in work and in life. Under her leadership, Dress for Success Central Virginia has served over 2500 women since 2012.

For her business acumen and nonprofit work, Shantell has been recognized by countless organizations including the National Association of Women Business Owners, Iota Phi Lambda Sorority, Omega Psi Phi Fraternity Inc., Yahoo! Women Who Shine, and Style Weekly Magazine as a 2012 Top 40 Under 40 Award Recipient.

Shantell received her Bachelor of Science in Business Administration from Virginia Commonwealth University, her Master of Business Administration from Strayer University, and her PhD in Organizational Management from Capella University all with specializations in Human Resource Management and Organizational Development. She is also a graduate of Nonprofit Learning Point's Emerging Nonprofit Leaders program and holds a Certificate in Fund Development from the University of Richmond.

Reclaiming My Power
Stacy Crawley

It was the summer of 1995 and I had just turned 10 years old. My cousins and I were hanging out over my grandmother's house as we did every year during this time. We were so excited because Earl, one of the homeless men in the neighborhood, would open the fire hydrant at least once a week so we could have fun and cool down. There were block parties, plus we skated up and down grandma's street (but not past Ms. Gloria's house, of course), played games like Tag, Freeze Tag, Mother May I, and Hide and Seek. I mean we had a ball every summer.

On Mondays, we couldn't wait to see Aunt MaryAnn come cruising through the alley near Grandma's house to pick us up and take us to our three favorite places. All of us, including Grandma, would pile into Aunt MaryAnn's burgundy Dodge minivan and start our day at Shoney's restaurant for breakfast, then horseback riding in Waldorf, and finally the thrift store in Camp Springs, MD, which was my grandma's favorite spot. We were in heaven!

It was Antwon, Donta, Tawanna, Markus, Monique, sometimes Maurice, and me. I remember this particular summer as if it were yesterday because it was one of the worst for me. It was the summer that I became public enemy number one. Every day turned into a "clown Stacy kind of day." It was the summer that I started to feel horrible about myself. I guess out of boredom, my cousins started taunting me on a consistent basis. I would hear things like, "you're fat," "you're ugly," "you'll never have a boyfriend," and "you're weird." This was new to me, and I didn't know how to handle it, nor did I tell my mom or my grandma what was going on. I suffered in silence.

One day it had gotten so bad, I started to feel depressed. Luckily, my mom had gotten off work early and picked me up. I couldn't wait to get home. When we arrived, I waited until my mom went into her room and I stood in the bathroom mirror staring at myself. I looked down at my stomach, then at my saggy arms, and put my hands up to my puffy face and I said, "they're right. You are ugly. You are fat and you'll never fit in." From that day, I started to believe everything my cousins had said to me. That night I thought to myself, "maybe if you're not here anymore, just maybe if you take your own life, then you will no longer feel the pain you've felt for so long." When I decided that was no longer an option, I started to resent my cousins and myself.

Meanwhile, the summer had ended, but the taunting continued for years and didn't stop until I reached high school. Although it wasn't as bad as before, the damage had already been done. I felt worthless. Even into my adulthood, I questioned everything I did and downplayed my abilities. I compared myself to other people and never really felt comfortable in my own skin. I lacked self-confidence and my self-esteem was non-existent, which was prime breeding ground to attract that same type of energy into my life in the form of a romantic partnership. During this relationship, I was devalued, disrespected, degraded, and made fun of. I was so broken that I had found myself in an abusive relationship -

one where my opinion and voice were muted, my emotional and mental health was trampled on, and my physical safety was jeopardized. Let's just say, I continued to sink deeper and deeper into depression.

Can I tell you that it got worse after I had my twins? I had experienced the worst case of postpartum depression and anxiety than my previous two child births. I felt like my baby girls deserved someone better than me, because I had convinced myself that somehow, I wasn't doing or being enough for them. I compared myself to other moms on social media who seemed to have it altogether. I mean, going from two to four kids overnight was no easy feat. I continued to suffer in silence.

I screamed, hollered, cried, and cried some more…I had mom rage. My hormones were completely out of whack and yet again, those feelings of not wanting to be here began to set in. "My girls will be fine. They have family who love them and will take good care of them. They won't miss me," I thought to myself one night.

That same night as the girls slept, I was sitting on the sofa when I heard God's voice say to me, "why can't you see yourself the way I see you?" Instantly, the tears began to flow. It was in that moment that I knew my life needed to change.

After having a heated discussion with my then husband about my depression and anxiety, I decided to seek help from my therapist who suggested that I go on a "momcation" to relax, reset, and recharge. I took that time to focus on just me, myself, and I. I was able to let my guard and my bra down and just be Stacy for a change. It was an amazing experience that I desperately needed, but it didn't cure the depression and anxiety that I was feeling.

So, after my "momcation," I had an appointment with my OB-GYN who I opened up to about what I was feeling and he suggested that I take anti-anxiety medication to help recalibrate my hormones and get back to feeling like myself. After staring at him for a solid fifteen seconds, I assured him that I didn't need any medication and that I would just pray my depression and anxiety away. Yet, he reassured me that I wouldn't have to be on it long and that it would greatly benefit me so I begrudgingly accepted the prescription. Thankfully within just a few weeks, I started to feel like myself again and I was so grateful. I felt a sense of relief as if the chains of depression and anxiety I had carried for so long were finally broken.

Through this journey, God made me realize that, "my story, as hard and hurtful as it was, was about me, but it wasn't for me." I realized that I was destined for more and even in my pain, this was my blessing. I knew in that moment that I had a life-changing message to share and that my dream of becoming a motivational speaker, author and coach was my divine purpose.

And today, I'm so thankful and proud to stand in my power and confidently say that I no longer feel broken, depressed, or less than. I feel beautiful (inside and out), stronger, blessed and highly favored.

If I can leave you anything, I want to share with you the three things I did that helped me to climb out of the hole of despair, depression and anxiety where I dwelled for so long...

(1.) **Be "still"**

    * With all that we have going on in our daily lives, it's hard to "be still." But in order to gain clarity, you must be

silent and listen for God's voice. When my girls would go to sleep at night, I would turn off my TV and my phone and it would be just me and my thoughts. I also prayed and meditated a lot. And let me tell you, through this process, I gained a sense of clarity I hadn't ever known before and it felt great.

(2.) **Seek help**

* Yes, we are strong, phenomenal, and resilient women; however, we're not superheroes. I had to learn that it's okay to ask for help when you're feeling down, broken, depressed, and/or overwhelmed. Whether you reach out to your close family members and friends or a therapist, don't be afraid to be vulnerable enough to be open and let people know where you stand mentally and emotionally. And if medication is offered, don't be so quick to turn it down. Do your research and make the best decision for your family. I did!

(3.) **Change the way I was thinking**

*I needed to change how I thought about myself and started telling the woman in my mirror how beautiful and wonderful she is. One day I decided to write down 10 positive affirmations about myself on sticky notes (i.e. you're beautiful, you're strong, you're enough, etc.). I put them up around my bathroom so that every time I looked in my mirror, I was reminded of how important, unique, and amazing I really was.

For once in my life, I started to feel joy, peace and genuine happiness.

So, how about you? Do you ever have moments where you feel less than or not good enough? Do you compare yourself and your life to other people's? Are you struggling with depression and anxiety?

- If this sounds familiar, I challenge you to...
    - Give yourself some grace and realize how wonderful you really are.
    - Be careful what you're telling the woman in your mirror.
    - Be kind and gentle to her, because she needs you.
    - Write down positive affirmations and post them where you see them constantly and draw from them when you need them the most.
    - Understand that no matter what, you will face trials and tribulations in life, but just know that you are more than enough. You are fierce, you are strong, you are destined for greatness, and you deserve nothing but God's best for your life!

Stacy S. Crawley *is a dynamic and passionate Motivational Speaker and Empowerment Coach who's adamant about impacting and transforming the lives of purpose-driven women all around the world by sharing her own personal trials and triumphs.*

As a mom of four beautiful girls and a domestic violence survivor, Stacy is no stranger to experiencing low self-esteem, low self-confidence, negative self-talk, self-doubt, limiting beliefs, depression and anxiety. However, that has not kept her from boldly pursuing her purpose or becoming the woman God has called her to be.

Stacy does a great job of providing practical tips, strategies, and relevant personal life experiences to help her audiences and clients reclaim their power, ignite their confidence, and fearlessly share their unique gifts with the world.

Stacy is the CEO and founder of Ignite Her Purpose, LLC.

Acknowledgements

Dr. LaToya Wiggins
She is Nourished, LLC
www.sheisanourishedmom.com
Facebook: @sheisanourishedmom
Instagram: @sheisanourishedmom
LinkedIn.com/in/sheisanourishedmom

Dallas Gordon
Journal Junk Box
Journaljunkbox.com
Facebook: @dgjournalco
Instagram: @dgjournalco

Christine Lawrence
Facebook: @Christine Lawrence
Instagram: @c.lawerence.mkibc

Nicole Reid
Poplar Creek Interiors
www.poplarcreekinteriors.com
Instagram: @thepoplarcreekco

Rosita Calderon
Rosey Designs
www.roseydesigns.co
Instagram: @roseydesigns.co

Marsha Canada

Danielle Armstrong
Studio 6414 Designs
Instagram: @studio_314_designs

Keana Lewis

Barbara Milton

Mary Williams

Shantelle Isaac
Facebook: Shantelle Mcneil
Instagram: @Telleshanie

Dave Crawley, Sr.

Nyteisha Stith
Thrivestudiollc
www.thrivestudiollc.com
Facebook: @nyteishanicole.stith
Instagram: @thrivestudiollc
LinkedIn.com/in/nyteisha-stith-632822157

Casandra Chamblis
Chamblis Consulting, LLC
Chamblisconsulting.com
Facebook: Casandra Chamblis
Instagram: @akapearl19
LinkedIn.com/in/chamblisconsulting

Healing Beyond the Veil
Joi Donaldson

What do you do when the tears taste familiar? When the blood coursing through you has seen these veins before, in another body, in another timeline? I envision an army of Black women, all in white, lining her body when they called my mother home. They look regal yet exhausted, saying without words that another has passed before the curse could lay at their feet. I recognize all and none of them. One twisting her machete against her palm. Another staring down every demon that dared try to lay strike to this occasion. My mother cracked the deeper realm before she knew she was gone. But I felt her leave years ago. The body she carried was finally told to rest.

They say dead men tell no tales, yet the voices of my dead folk speak loudly. The women that line the wall above my ancestor altar come from a pain that sinks below their surface. I still hear their muted laughs, remember the mundane moments of folding line-dried clothes together, sitting between my grandmother's knees as she drew her part into my head. I sit at my altar similar in body, music from my playlist wafting between this veil and the next. I set a tone, adopt a posture similar to the one that bent me forward after hearing the news of her passing. I was so far away and she was alone for we don't know how long. It's a tragic beauty to know the end before it comes and choose to let it play out as it's the only way to move us toward the light. I march along these days after greeting her at the altar. She used to stick out but now she feels at home. My altar is peaceful; before it was loud, disturbed, angry.

The depression that lines the fabric of my family lineage is thick. It touches each of us differently. Some by self-medicating, some with toxicity in relationships, some through vices that surface fiercely early or later in life. Navigating the dust that settles after a depressive break included fully negating the emotions that fell. It was being strong, lifting up while bleeding, lost limbs and sour tongues. Depression made itself at home within the spaces we forgot to clean and grew bigger and more formidable. It greeted us at family functions when the liquor began to flow and the memories became fuzzy. My mother was one of those who hid her depression in plain sight. I had the audacity to be the walking mirror she fought to avoid: broken shards made up our relationship. I shared space with her and her depression on a nightly basis. Depression helped me pick her up from the floor after one too many. It helped me blow into her breathalyzer so we could get off that bridge and go home. It worked with me to push through homework that came with screaming and unhinged perfection. I adopted depression as my own as it felt like the only home I knew. When I didn't feel it on my chest once I opened my eyes, I felt lonely. As an only child, depression came with playmates: anxiety and later PTSD. My mother rocked us all to sleep with brown on her lips and the longing to give more but the inability to do so. When my ancestors spoke in 2016, sharing that she wouldn't be long for this world, I began my years of mourning. I pulled myself close whenever I called and it took a while for her to answer. My breath would catch in my chest when I heard her voice after a time of not speaking. "Is today the day?" became a familiar hymn. She left and depression added a new friend: grief.

Grief is a funny beast. It comes when you're walking through Target and feel your knees buckle at the sight of the air fryer your mom said she wanted. It tag-teams with depression brain to "help" you forget the things you wish to remember. My Black women in white surround me during those moments, fighting to crack through the walls mental unwellness have trapped me behind. Even deeper fighting to break the walls I've carved out on my own. When they get to me, I'm beneath the rubble. My nails are sunken in, my hands raw, my feet crushed. My throat caked in soot and cement. I try to speak and more curses leave my lips. It's what I've known: curse yourself so the curses of others hold no effect. My women tear from me the root of what ails me, the lessons my mother taught me as a failed approach to protection. I watch as they gnash and spit out the sourness of my words and break them underneath their feet. "You are not helpless," I hear as my body rises on its own. I see a little girl that looks like me running towards me. She hugs the crooks of my knees as she falls into me. Is this how freedom looks? Is this what depression, anxiety, grief, mourning, PTSD have stolen from me? How do we leave here together in one piece? I wonder.

There's beauty in the tragedy of a fallen monument to a life once known. There's life in the warranted death of what once held you hostage. What is a gilded cage but a pretty prison? What is pretending to be okay but another curse in the making? How often do we side with the oppressive notions that made the generations before us feel safe in the moment, only to destroy us later? The curses that lie beneath depression and anxiety make for the cruelest comforters. I'm frequent bedfellows with mourning and grief. We talk each other to sleep and wake around the same time. Anxiety comes through to remind me to do everything and nothing all at once. I crash later, struggling to remember how to take a full breath. I wish I knew the cure. I wish I knew how to salve a shipload of Black souls' sadness that they couldn't describe. A sadness that flows through generations with no true end in sight. There has to be life worth living beyond glory. There has to be a space where depression can be seen casket-sharp on this land, never to rise again. While we wait, what do we do?

I'm guided back to my vision of Black women in white. Their sleeves soft and withered, their necks strong, their teeth bright. They have the audacity to smile against the pain. To show up as crystal-clear technicolor against a wash of black and white. Blood red isn't the only color they know. A sea of Black, brown, indigenous beings take their places around me. I know these bodies, this skin, this pain. I don't swallow what isn't mine but drink down the lessons they were blocked from telling. I cry and meet depression again. It's smaller, less ravenous and ready to tear me apart. It sits back and admires, knowing as it visits from time to time, it won't be around long. The others gather around it, hunkering down for another whirlwind of promise, of fight, of calling back all that was stolen and returning it to the fertile ground from which it grew. In this space I sense her. I see my mother most in my dreams now. She's never known that level of peace while also forgetting she exists as spirit. She has been welcomed by those who left before her, reassuring her that it's okay to let go. That she won't be forgotten. It's odd to know she finds her healing through me now: the one so skilled at building monuments to agony. With the same hands she taught me she honors my unlearning. Our hands are similar. I used mine to nurse her wounds a couple weeks before she left. She allowed me to help her. I knew she was leaving soon. I've always been my mother's keeper. Now she gets to carry and keep me from the other side.

I speak my kinship with depression in order to drop the curtain shielding me from sanctuary. I tell about all the ways I've done its dirty work and how I continue to learn, unlearn and relearn. I take meds because I'm not ashamed. I draw blood when I need to through writing. I've taken up the mantle as curse breaker, and with that I count myself as tribute. I sing towards those who have been waiting for me. I hold space for those yet to come. I tell my child that their feelings are valid and depression, in particular, lies for a living. I have beef with all that tries to consume me and those I hold dear. My fight begins every day once my eyes meet the ceiling. It's a new day, a new song to my chorus, a new reason to wear white and to keep fighting.

Joi Donaldson

Joi Donaldson *is a 10x published author, sexuality professional, award-winning filmmaker, mental health advocate and all-around creative. She's a curator of good vibes and, through transparency and humor, has learned how to make tough conversations fun.*

I Fought My Way Back
Dr. Shonda Harris-Muhammed

Who will tell the dark generational secret of molestation, rape, physical and mental abuse if I am erased from this earth?

Growing up as a child without my father, I struggled to understand why I could not have a daddy to protect me, who I could love and who would love me back as I observed other little girls with their fathers. My father unfortunately died from cancer when I was just 18 months old.

When I was just a small child I was introduced to physical, mental, and sexual abuse. Men began taking advantage of me just as I was preparing for kindergarten. In addition to that, I endured many nights of hearing my mother scream through domestic disputes as if she was fighting for her life. Oftentimes, I witnessed my brother trying to intercede and do the best he could as a young man to protect his mother and sisters. For me, all three malevolent behaviors were equally horrifying. They served the same purpose: to kill and destroy. Eventually, my oldest brother became angry and bitter. I became lost in fear, devastated, crumbled in pain, and confused as to what was happening to me while my only sister positioned herself to protect me as best as she could. I wanted to die.

A man my mother was dating forced me to have oral sex with him consistently. Today, at 49 years old, I still do not understand what he could have possibly seen in a child. I was just a little girl in elementary school with thick, long pigtails desiring to have a father. Was this the behavior of all fathers in the world? Is this what all men did to little girls? Who in their right mind could do something so horrible to a child? I was confused as a child and was desperately trying to comprehend what was happening to me. This man destroyed my childhood from the day he forced me to engage inappropriately with him. I was a child for God's sake! "Shh, do not tell or I will kill your mom," he'd say. So I didn't tell. Who would know? Who would care? I felt deserted and helpless. This madness of behavior continued for many years and all I could do was force myself to think of another place to be. The constant hate I had for myself as a child due to not understanding what was happening to me and why no one was protecting me became more prevalent that I began to act out uncontrollably. I needed someone to save me. I only felt safe when I was with my grandparents who lived in Louisa County, Virginia. I constantly prayed that they would secretly drive to Chesapeake and force the door down, grab me, and take me away. That never happened; well, at least not in that manner.

The traumatic experiences imposed upon me by my mother's ex-lover plagued me for many years as a young adult. I felt vulnerable to men and didn't know or care about myself enough to love myself. I simply did not know how to do that. What was love? I was not loved enough to keep a grown man from having his way with me - whether in my mother's house, in a shed, or in a dark, deserted place. I wanted to die. Daddy, where are you? He wasn't there and he was not coming back to the 18-month-old baby girl he left. My life was not worth living. I found myself gasping for air, struggling to breathe in the same air that was keeping me alive. I was lost in a world filled with family members who thought they could have their way with me and no one would ever know. Yes, I also had family members touch me in places that were not acceptable! As a child I wanted to scream, "STOP TOUCHING ME!" I was determined to break free and try to make sense of why this was happening. I felt scared and lonely. My entire being illuminated into darkness. I handled life as if it was not worth living. Who would notice if I was gone? Where was my protection? I did not ask for any of this to happen to me. No matter how often I took baths, rinsed my mouth, or chewed bubble gum, I still felt filthy. I became depressed enough that I attempted suicide. I tried cutting my wrist. While attempting to cut my wrist I began to express to my inner self, *what will happen if there is a lot of blood? Do I cut it the long way or the short way? Should I write a note to my grandparents and tell them how much I love them and want to be with them? Should I tell my mom in the letter what I was going through? Should I take the community bus to church first and then do it? Maybe I should call 911 and let them know what is happening with me.* All of these thoughts and questions ran through my mind. Suddenly, in that moment I felt a strong presence over me. What was this feeling? I couldn't describe it. I was going through an out-of-body experience. Tears began to flow down my face and I realized that something, that presence that felt unnatural while natural, was a voice speaking to me. My daddy was with me. I laid on the floor and I prayed. I am here today because God kept me. Whew, God kept me even when I could not keep myself. While I was trying to destroy myself, my body, my spirit and mind, God spoke to me through my daddy on that day to say, "I got you baby."

Satiated with determination to live, I chose to fight back. One day soon after, I wrote in my AP Biology journal what was happening to me. My teacher reported it to my school counselor and my school counselor called the Department of Social Services. I knew when they called me to the office I was being saved from the hell I was living in. I knew I could make it another day. I knew someone would finally protect me. The abuse had matriculated for years. The physical beatings I witnessed my mother take consistently was overwhelming and I sought help, not just for myself, but for her too. How could a teenager be equipped to rescue herself and her mom? I did not have the answers but I knew as I was walking swiftly and courageously to the office that I would figure it out when I got there. When I arrived at the school counselor's office, I felt a strong sense that the adults standing at the door knew why I was there. Everyone smiled at me and said hello. One man could not take his eyes off me but it was not an uncomfortable stare. I felt it was an observance of "God has you." He just looked at me with a soft grin as if my daddy was within reminding me that he was still with me. I walked into the school counselor's office who actually was not my assigned school counselor. She served other students in other grades, but on this day, she was of service to me. That day, my auntie - my father's sister- was called. My dear auntie had to break the news to my grandparents that I was being sexually abused. I was told my papa stated, "we are going to get her." On that day, I found protection. And it was also on that day that my life changed forever.

I was determined to live. I reminded myself each day that I am loved and needed to learn how to love myself. I had to know and embrace love for myself: comfortable, honest, transparent, warm, healing, and that agape love. I grew stronger in the Lord while residing with my grandparents. I observed their service to the community and to our church. I was always with my grandparents in town at the Safeway Supermarket or the State Fair. Wherever they were, so was I. When I was with my grandparents, I felt safe and they always fed me - not with just edible items, but with love. I am who I am today because of the grace and promises God has bestowed upon me to survive and walk in the vastness that I have. I am no longer a victim of abuse; I am a conqueror through Christ Jesus. Because of the blood of Jesus, I can live.

Philippians 4:13: I can do all things in Christ who strengthens me.

One of the most challenging things in life is to face the hurt, disgust, betrayal and pain of one's past. It is very difficult to focus on the imminent when you are still dealing with unresolved issues of your past. Breaking free from my nightmare of a past did not break me from facing the pain. I found strength in my faith: a topic my grandparents discussed with me often. I remember my grandmother telling me in her soft sweet voice, "before you can face your struggles, you must deal with God. You got to get it right with God, Shon Poo." She prayed over me and shouted "enemy, this one you will not have!" I laid my head on her lap while she rubbed my hair and my face. "God has my baby girl. He has you honey. I love you and God loves you too." The breakthrough was distorted but I knew it was inward. I had an intercessor.

From that point on, I knew I would have to deal with the sexual and mental abuse I encountered as a young child through my early teenage years. I knew that I needed to forgive my mom for the hurt and mistrust I formed in my heart for her. For many years I struggled to form healthy relationships with women who tried to help me in school because of the pain I was silently dealing with. I was making them pay for the pain and hurt I received from a man my mother dated. See, I blamed my mom for everything that happened to me. I blamed my mom for the family members who thought they could touch me and the people who turned a blind eye. I blamed my mom for the nightmares and the lack of self-discipline with men and the lack of self-respect I had absorbed. But God. Forgiveness was essential so I could live. My son taught me that. I had to come face-to-face with God and my pain. I needed to be broken so I could be repaired again. My spiritual father, my former pastor, was a beacon of light in my life who helped me through counseling to deal with my unresolved issues. Therapy is not an unpleasant word. I found healing through counseling and therapy sessions. In those sessions I discovered who I was.

As life progressed, my children and my faith combined with joy and strength also helped me discover who I am. From my husband, I learned mindfulness and adoring myself like no other can. I can actually love and be loved no matter my past filled with guilt, filth, and struggle of wanting to survive. I was being loved and it felt like a breakthrough. I had to get right with God in order for me to see who God is for me. My relationship with Christ opened the door to peace that passes all understanding and the courage to face my guilt and pain. God has been and continues to be a very present help in my time of need. He was with me when I was being abused. He was with me when I wanted to die. He is with me now! I am FREE because of the blood of Jesus. I am FREE!

"When you have been covered in the blood of the Lamb, it's all good!"- Dr. Mary Hallums, my former Doctoral Chair and forever Godsent mentor

Dr. Shonda M. Harris-Muhammed, *also affectionately known as Dr. HM, is a 30-year educator, wife, and mother of two children who bring great joy to her life. For 14 years, she has provided free school supplies and other resources to the children and teachers in the Richmond, VA area through her nonprofit, Northside Coalition for Children, Inc. Dr. Shonda was raised in a town called Cuckoo, Virginia in Louisa County where her grandparents raised her with a tremendous amount of love, protection and support.*

I Fought My Way Back

As a survivor of molestation and rape, Dr. Shonda has been determined all her adult life to protect and educate families and her students about the impact of sexual, mental, and physical abuse. Currently, she serves as the School Board Chair and representative to the Sixth District on the Richmond School Board. She is also a member of Alpha Kappa Alpha Sorority, Inc., a charter member of BWEl - Black Women Educator Leaders, and she currently serves as a trustee of her church. Her favorite scripture is Philippians 4:13: I can do ALL things in Christ who strengthens me. She lives by this verse every day while providing support to the communities she serves.

Dr. Shonda currently resides in Southern Barton Heights with her college sweetheart, her husband Demetrius.

Acknowledgements

Gloria H. Yates
My Next Act Realty
Facebook: @gloria.yates.77

Latosha Branch
https://www.facfacebook.com/profile.php?id=100004572019057
Instagram: @branchlatosha

Michelle Mosby
Help Me Help You Foundation
Hmhyfoundation.org
Facebook: @helpmehelpyoufdn
Instagram: @helpmehelpyoufdn

Deaconess Ethel Green
Bethlehem Baptist Church
https://www.mybbcfairmount.org/

Tracy E. Callwood
Instagram: @Bizgal
LinkedIn.com/in/tracy-e-callwood-1844a168

Sheila Phillips
Facebook.com/lenna.richards.9

Nicole Jackson

Rhonda Chambliss
Retired Educational Administrator
Facebook: @rhondalee
Instagram: @hamptonmade
LinkedIn.com/in/rhondachamblisse

Anthony Harris-Muhammed

Demetrius Muhammed

Khadijah Harris-Muhammed

Sheila Phillips

Deaconess Jackie Webster

BODIES In BOXES
Andrea "Aj" Sanders

Now I Lay Me Down To Sleep, I Pray the Lord My Soul To Keep, If I Should Die Before I Wake, I Pray the Lord My Soul To Take...

"Come on, hurry child! Stop playing with that doll. Get dressed. We have to go soon."

I loved getting dressed up in my white dress and patent leather shoes, carrying my pocketbook just like Momma. I asked Momma why we were getting dressed up - it wasn't Sunday - but Momma didn't answer. I didn't know why she looked so sad and why she was crying so many days leading up to now. It was Friday - a hot day and the big fan was on. It seemed like all the people on our block were at our house, even mean old Ms. Mattie. Everyone brought all kinds of food, from fried chicken, to potato salad, greens, biscuits, pies and cakes, covered in tin foil and smelling good. I had never seen so much food and I was excited! We must be having a party, I thought! Usually when we have a lot of food, Momma cooks it and she is happy, but today she looked sad and no one was staying for the party. They just dropped off food, hugged Momma, and some cried as they left.

"Hurry child, hurry," Momma said again. "They are waiting for us to get in the car." Grabbing my hand tightly, Momma practically dragged me out the front door where this big, long, shiny black car was parked. A man all dressed in black opened the car door and we got in. I had never seen such a big car with so many seats in it. Auntie and Uncle were in the car and some lady I didn't know. Momma and Auntie hugged and started crying. The car slowly pulled off and I heard Auntie say, "We must stop crying. We must be strong." Then she started crying harder. I was sad and scared. I had never seen Momma and Auntie cry before. I wondered why we left home, left all the food and where we were going.

The car drove us to this place I had never been before. We went in and a lot of people were there all dressed up in black too. We walked to the front of the room and stopped in front of this pretty pink and white looking bed. I had to stand on my tippy toes to see. I had so many questions. "Momma, why is Grandma sleeping? She looks pretty. Is she going to get out of the bed and come to our house for the party?"

"Shhhhhhhh child, be quiet," Momma said as we went to sit down in chairs in front of Grandma. Momma started shaking and crying loudly. Auntie was hollering, praying, and asking God why. I looked around and noticed I was the only child there dressed in my pretty white dress that Grandma bought for my birthday.

I was used to Grandma always giving me hugs and kisses and also making Momma happy but today she didn't say a word. She just laid in this bed, smiling, with her eyes closed. She never sat up to hug me. I started crying like Momma and Auntie because Grandma wouldn't look at me. After a long time, a lot of songs and prayers, Momma stopped crying and I asked her why Grandma was still sleeping. Momma leaned over and whispered, "Grandma is not going to ever wake up again. Grandma is in heaven."

I remember this as if it were yesterday. I was six years old. They put a blanket over my Grandma, Momma kissed her and then they closed up the pretty bed that looked like a big, long box. We left Grandma's body in that box, and I never saw my Grandma, or got one of her big hugs and kisses, again. By the time I was twelve years old, seven more people I loved, including Momma, were placed in boxes and I was a depressed child.

Childhood depression was unheard of back then. Children were to do as they were told, ask no questions, stay out of grown folks' business, and behave. Truth be told, depression was not something working class people, especially poor black and brown people, had time for. Sadness, the blues, and feelings of weariness were noticed, acknowledged, and attempts to make things better existed for adults. However, that deep dark pain that hurts all over, that makes you feel as if the world is closing in around you, and you can't breathe, can't face another day, or get out of bed was called everything but depression. That pain was, and still is, dealt with by self-medicating with alcohol, food, drugs, sex, shopping, stealing, gambling, workaholism, sleeping, verbal, emotional and physical abuse of others and self, sexual abuse, being funny, trying to please everyone all the time, isolating, addiction to social media, committing acts of crime and violence, and plain old denial. Sadly, depression sets in very young, and is the result of, and triggered by, traumatic life events. When left unaddressed, childhood depression leads to severe adult depression and suicide, now more than ever.

Death and dying seemed like such a morbid subject to write about but desperately needs attention. My early childhood losses due to the deaths of loved ones left me frightened, sad, angry, and orphaned. I had no one to talk to about how scared I was about dying and having my body placed in a box. There was no conversation at the dinner table or in school about dying and death. There was only the pain of goodbyes and those sayings I came to hate: "So and so was a good, God-fearing person who is in a better place. They are in heaven now. No more pain, no more suffering. Or worse, that they might or should rot in hell!"

After each death I worried when it would be my turn to be placed in a box, in the ground, and if I would make it into heaven. When I was a little girl, it seemed only grown-ups died. When Momma died, I was only twelve. She was pretty and only twenty-nine and that's when I became really depressed. From then on, I lived in silent fear that I also would not live longer than 29 years old and dreaded every birthday. I was sad and scared all the time. I was called moody, a problem child or weird. No one understood. No one was listening to what I was feeling. No one heard me screaming out for help. If they listened for a moment, they chose to ignore the red flags of depression most children exhibit. I began to self-medicate with books, eating, not eating, sleeping, and isolating. I also began scribbling poems on tiny pieces of paper and napkins expressing pain, sadness and hopelessness and creating this fantasy world of happiness that didn't exist. When forced to live in the real world I was the ultimate happy positive person and people pleaser. It felt good making others happy, taking care of others, bringing joy, and showing up confident, strong and ready to conquer the world all the while hiding the pain and sadness I woke up with and went to sleep with every day. When I dared to try and talk to someone about my feelings it made matters worse. I was told by loving, caring adults… "Be strong, just don't think about death. That's just life - here today, gone tomorrow. You'll get over it; toughen up, pray about it."

Martin Luther King, Jr. was murdered on my birthday. Kids started murdering each other in the streets. Friends left for Vietnam and died. Serial killers became famous on the news and mass murders started.

Please know our children are listening. They have no choice as social media, the news and adult conversations speak of death and dying all the time. Today as I write this chapter four mass murders have flooded the news in the last three weeks, killing innocent children in school, shoppers in grocery stores and people in a medical center. Most of the killing is done by young, angry, hurting, mentally ill and emotionally unstable boys and men! Special attention is needed for depressed boys who are taught very young not to cry, show emotions, be afraid or show weakness. They are told to 'man up' by those who love them the most! Holding all their emotions inside leads to sadness, fear, anger, and depression that has to come out. We no longer feel safe going to concerts, places of worship, the movies, or to college and the suicide rate among children is at an all-time high. The impact of depression in children undiagnosed, untreated, and misunderstood is destroying lives, families, and communities. Our children are traumatized by all the death and dying in their neighborhoods and in the world. They have to keep watching their friends die and are severely depressed because of it. They are committing suicide to escape the pain, dark thoughts, and sense of hopelessness because of so much death. Self-medicating amongst children these days is the same as adults. We must stop ignoring childhood depression that leads to severe adult depression. Start listening, paying attention, and start helping our children. We must stop ignoring the red flags and stop dismissing obvious and subtle behaviors and comments expressed by those depressed.

In a recent conversation with children ages five to twelve (some diagnosed with ADHD), regarding the killing of children in schools and death and dying, their questions and comments were startling. They wondered if death hurts and who made it to Heaven and hell. They said they probably would die by sixteen and listed several young friends and family members who died by murder or suicide. Most frightening of all, they said death and suicide were things they thought about a lot when they didn't feel happy. Those age ten and up said that death by suicide would be better than living and feeling sad, scared, alone, bullied and not liked. Most had never had a conversation with their parents or a responsible adult about their thoughts and feelings. These kids are all depressed and need our help.

As a little girl who stood in front of her grandma's body in a box, with no understanding of what was going on and no adults to understand, I shouldn't have been there. Perhaps if I hadn't, I would not have grown up to be afraid of death and dying, resulting in depression.

How do I deal with death, dying and depression now and the constant images of bodies in boxes? Glad you asked. Please take note and help children do the same.

1) Prayer

2) Talking about my feelings

3) Therapy

4) Exercising

5) Eating healthy

6) Managing self-medicating behaviors

7) Asking for help until someone listens

And the belief that we are spiritual beings living on this earth for a short time with a purpose!

Prayer alone is not enough. Therapy alone is not enough. Exercising alone is not enough. Eating healthy alone is not enough and talking about my feelings alone is not enough! Depression is a serious medical condition triggered by many things that need many different healing methods simultaneously, including prescription depression medicine when diagnosed as clinically depressed.

Depression is the result of many things in children. Please help our children so that they stop bullying, killing others and committing suicide because they are feeling hopeless, scared, angry, lonely, and misunderstood…because they are depressed. Yes, those who bully are depressed about something, one of the biggest red flags of depression in children. I am not writing this as a trained therapist, psychologist, psychiatrist, or mental health expert. I am sharing this as one who suffered with childhood and now adult depression around the subject of death and dying, who works hard to manage it almost daily, with all the news of death and dying every day, everywhere. My hope and my prayer is that one day soon there will be fewer bodies in boxes as the result of untreated depression that starts very young due to this rarely discussed topic.

And so, I close with the childhood prayer I opened with, taught to me by my grandmother. I said this prayer on my knees each night before going to sleep, before they placed her body in that box, and before death and dying made me depressed with a bit of a twist…

Now I lay me down to sleep, I pray the Lord all souls to keep

and if we die before we wake, I pray the Lord all souls He takes

BODIES In BOXES

I pray that children can live in peace,

that murder, suicide, and depression cease

and bodies in boxes don't increase

because depression in children is recognized, diagnosed, treated

and begins to decrease.

Amen!

Dedicated to all suffering with the fear and hurt of death and dying and who are depressed, especially children.

A special thanks to my loving husband, Rev. Dr. Michael A. Sanders, and Dear Sister-Friend, Mrs. Lisa Steinberg, who loves me through the highs and lows and encourages me to live when most afraid of dying!

Andrea "Aj" Sanders *is President and Co-Founder of Aj Sanders Training & Consulting, LLC, an author and First Lady of Christian Ministries Beyond Walls where her husband, Rev. Dr. Michael A. Sanders, is the Pastor.*

Andrea "Aj" Sanders

Aj and her team have successfully provided coaching and consulting services throughout the United States, Africa and the Caribbean. Satisfied clients include houses of faith, hospitals, social services and Fortune 500 organizations. Previously, Aj held leadership and staff development positions at The National Aquarium in Baltimore, Norfolk Convention & Visitors Bureau, the Marriott and Sheraton Hotels.

Aj is most experienced in coaching leaders and teams, serving those in need of spiritual, physical, psychological, and emotional healing. She has studied at the University of Pittsburgh, Temple University and received a full scholarship from the Smithsonian Diversity Leadership Training Institute in Washington, D.C. She is also a Certified Executive and Personal Life Coach.

No More Running
Dr. Tabatha M. W. Spurlock

"Cast all your anxiety on him because he cares for you."
1 Peter 5:7

I was sitting at my desk at work when I received an email about a volunteer opportunity from the assistant superintendent. Central office staff members were asked to participate in a reading initiative at elementary schools across our district. I immediately signed up to be a volunteer reader. As a parent of an elementary-aged child, I definitely wanted to give back to our neighborhood school.

October 27, 2016 arrived and I was excited to read to the children! I put on a cute outfit with a pair of matching heels; however, I changed my mind minutes before leaving the house. I thought "it's a group of first graders and I can be more casual." I opted for a pair of brown, leather riding boots instead and quickly ditched the heels. I arrived at the elementary school, pulled into a parking space and sat in my car for a few minutes to gather my thoughts and pray. I was ready to empower a group of young minds, but I never made it into the building.

As I walked from my car in the maze-like parking lot, a fellow parent driving an SUV ran me over. Moments later, I was lying on the ground unable to move my legs without discomfort. My pantyhose were torn with blood exposed from visible scarring on both legs. My leather boots were scratched up on both feet and I was perplexed as to what had just happened. My purse had flown out of my hand a few feet away from me. It was a struggle, but I managed to reach it to grab my phone. I yelled to the woman who hit me "CALL THE POLICE" as she stood outside of her SUV with her phone in her hand in shock as well. I called my husband, who was literally around the corner, and told him to come to the school.

The police arrived minutes later and I was rushed to the emergency room for my first ambulance experience of my life. A few family members and my boss met us at the hospital for support. After the doctor reviewed my x-rays, the diagnoses included a sprained neck, leg, and ankle. I was sent home with a note to return to work within three days along with a referral to see an orthopedic in five days for further evaluation. I was provided a pair of crutches for walking and my husband proceeded to take me home.

I could not stand up without being in excruciating pain and the crutches were not an easy feat. By the time we arrived home, my emotions were all over the place. It hurt to get out of the car and we struggled going up the steps trying to avoid falling. Every movement thereafter felt like an unbearable task. I knew in my gut that my sustained injuries were more severe than a sprain. At my visit to the orthopedic a few days later, he concluded I suffered a tibia plateau fracture (TPF) and surgery was required within two weeks. As he spoke, my heart dropped and there were uncontrollable tears running down my face. I immediately felt like a failure to my daughter because this meant we would have to postpone a trip I had promised her a month prior. The mommy guilt was real and overwhelming.

Over the next three months, I had to learn how to adjust by using a wheelchair, crutches and finally, I graduated into a brace. However, the first 40 days were the most trying as I was confined to the first floor of our home. I was in a non-weight bearing status and my physical therapist would come to our home a few times per week for treatment. At the 40-day mark, I was able to navigate my way up and down the 16 steps in our home. I was excited to be back in my own bed again. The hospital bed that had temporarily taken up residence in our family room had to go. Shortly thereafter, I transitioned from in-home to outpatient PT. It felt so good to get out of the house again even if it was for therapy.

I was able to return to work after three months, but something just didn't feel right. As I passed colleagues in the hall, on the elevator, and in the parking lot, the million dollar question couldn't be avoided: "Are you ok?" And my accustomed response was "yes, I'm ok," knowing I was on the verge of an emotional breakdown. I didn't recognize myself anymore. My colleagues didn't know it, but I would hide in my office most days with my door closed in avoidance of others. I didn't want or like all of the newfound attention, but there was one sweet lady whose desk was near the restroom who made me smile. She was more mature and had a way of making me feel good in my broken state.

By summer, I was definitely feeling like someone else. Ladies, I went for the one thing that we do to let others know something's going on. I cut my hair and I also became withdrawn from others not feeling like the go-getter I was prior to the accident. Alas, I scheduled an appointment with a psychologist to determine what was happening to me. I couldn't run from it anymore. In that session, he diagnosed me with post-traumatic stress disorder (PTSD), anxiety, and depression. I was not surprised at all from the research I had conducted based upon my symptoms and emotions at the time.

I was suffering and didn't know what to do. I was denied mental health support by my worker's compensation adjuster. She nor her superiors felt that I needed any treatment beyond physical therapy. I asked God repeatedly to make it make sense because I couldn't understand how I wasn't supposed to be mentally and emotionally affected by the aftermath of an accident. How was I supposed to deal with the trauma? Within a week of the diagnosis, I quit my "dream job" after only serving in that capacity for two years. It took me 10 years, starting out as a classroom teacher, to earn the central office position. But, I wasn't ok and didn't really know how to ask for help. As a strong friend and family member, some people left me to figure things out on my own while others saw through my attempts of isolation. "How do I cope and survive?" were the main things on my mind. And, since the system wasn't willing to give me the support I needed, I was forced to put my own self-care plan in place.

By this time, my stepson had moved out of the house so we had an extra bedroom. I changed the bedrooms around moving our daughter into his old room and I inherited her old bedroom as my new war room. It was my safe place that I could retreat to when I felt overwhelmed and needed a quiet place to rest my mind. I picked back up with writing my dissertation so it was the perfect place for late night grinding while researching and writing. I had decided enough was enough and it was time to stop running! I eventually learned how to cope and survive from day to day and you can too! Here's how:

Pray - I know God got tired of me asking Him, "Why me? Why did You put me in that place at that time for my life to be changed forever?" His reply, "Jeremiah 29:11." He knew that I wouldn't sit on my story. He knew, when I didn't even know, how I would overcome this traumatic situation. He knew that my own healing journey would lead to healing for others. Every time I tell my story, I can't help but give God all of the glory for where I am today.

Secure a safe space - I shared this tip already and it's worth the reminder.

Smile - In the midst of it all, don't lose your smile. It doesn't mean that you're not hurting. It just means that you desire to become better and not bitter as you fight through the pain.

Show up for yourself - It took me two years, but I was finally awarded mental health support from my former employer. The downside, I ended up losing the award due to malpractice by my attorney. That's another story for another book! The point is that I fought for myself inside and outside of courtrooms! I also wrote a best-selling children's book, *A Promise is a Promise*, to help myself and other moms conquer mommy guilt.

Others often say to me "you don't look like what you've been through" after hearing my story. I would say that is a true statement. When I think about all that the Lord has brought me through, I can't help but smile and be grateful. My new personal motto is "My life is not my own." My gifts are meant to be shared with others, including my story, and I hope you will join me on this "no more running" journey.

Dr. Tabatha Spurlock *is a wife, mother, entrepreneur, 3X best-selling author, philanthropist, highly energetic motivational speaker, and educator for over 15 years. She also volunteers with several community organizations and enjoys serving as a mentor and board member for a nonprofit organization called MEGA Mentors. This leader has a true servant's heart and desire to help uplift, motivate, and inspire others.*

No More Running

In 2016, she was the victim of a traumatic accident that left her unable to walk unassisted for three months. Over the years, she's had to learn how to conquer her diagnoses of PTSD, anxiety, and depression. While the journey has been extremely challenging at times, she has learned how to bounce back from life's setbacks with ease. She is no longer running from the trauma and pain. She's using her voice to help inspire and empower others.

Acknowledgements

Shereá Burnett
ThisWomansWords
www.thiswomanswords.co
Facebook: @ShereáDenise
Instagram: @shereadenise
www.linkedin.com/in/shereadburnett

The Power of Vulnerability
Tiffany Winfield

I was 38 and my divorce was pending from an almost 20 year relationship. Nine of those 20 years were spent married. Our relationship was never a fairytale but the spectators looking from the outside in would probably say otherwise. I loved my husband, but I should have never married as young as I did. I wasn't ready. I didn't have the opportunity to get to know myself and learn what truly makes me happy. All I cared about was that he loved me, he came from a great family, and by marrying him I would not be single and alone which was my biggest fear. At the time, I thought *who would want to be with a divorced woman suffering from depression, anxiety and PTSD*. In addition to my pending divorce, my sister was on dialysis seven days a week and eight hours a day. It was the summer of 2019 when she was diagnosed with stage five kidney failure, also referred to as renal failure. It progressed rapidly in a matter of a few months. I recalled the day my sister and my mom were both admitted to the hospital on the same day in two different cities, two and a half hours apart from each other. Talk about making a calculated choice of who you're going to go be with. Mom it was.

My mom has Cognitive Dementia and has suffered from diabetes for over 40 years. Her health deteriorated rapidly. Just as fast as my sister's kidney failure. My sister and I made the hardest choice of our lives and decided to move our mom out of the only home she knew for 40 plus years. Several nursing home visits later, we landed on the one we thought would be best for her. I would have never thought the day my mom and sister were both hospitalized, that my mom would never step foot back into her house. She went to rehabilitation for a few weeks after a surgery that then required a life-long colostomy bag, then to her permanent residence at that same nursing facility in December 2019. Of course, I didn't know that the COVID-19 pandemic would arise which prohibited me from physically seeing my mom for a whole year and three months. The guilt of placing my mom in a nursing facility was heavy, but to go more than a year and not be able to touch her was a nightmare.

Fast forward to October 2020, after almost a year and a half under the same roof with my then soon to be ex-husband, I had finally moved into my brand new townhouse which I purchased on my own with no down payment required. My credit score was damn near perfect. I was promoted and received a 12% increase in my pay four months prior at my job. I had no debt other than my house and student loans. I was financially secure and my divorce was almost finalized. My sister was finally getting her new kidney from a living donor and my mom, for the moment, was peacefully situated in the nursing home and receiving the care that I physically could not give to her. Despite the death grip that COVID-19 had on humanity, I traveled internationally and was able to remain free of the virus unlike others that I knew. But life's circumstances, my mistakes, shame, regrets, and generational curses seemed to have a chokehold around my neck. Years of depression and anxiety had infested my mental space and any light in my soul was consumed by the darkness of my mental illness.

The Power of Vulnerability

Regardless of every blessing that God was sending my way, life was the worst thing ever and I had reached my breaking point.

I laid in the middle of my kitchen floor in the fetal position, questioning my entire life. Reflecting on every single mistake I ever made. I was mad that the suicide attempt at age 16 didn't work. That was the attempt which would have saved me from years of self-hatred, feeling unlovable, and having no self-esteem. It would have saved me years of having daddy issues and looking for a man who could replace my father and love me unconditionally just like he did. I have always suppressed the grief of my father's unexpected death and never processed it fully to this day. There were two other attempts about a year or so ago that sure as hell didn't go as planned. My car is still scratched up from the day I attempted to drive into the James River then abruptly, what I call, punked out. I was so pissed at myself for not taking myself out sooner.

Earlier that day, prior to me laying out on the kitchen floor, I had strategically updated all beneficiaries on my assets and insurance policies. I texted my sister all the information she needed to be able to handle my affairs after I was gone. I sent her my life insurance and banking information as well as a list of where all of my assets were distributed. She never caught on to why I did that. I figured she wouldn't anyway. Everything was all set.

I lethargically made my way upstairs to my bathroom and collapsed on the floor. I pressed my face against the cold tile. It felt soothing in a weird way. My face and shirt were soaking wet from all the tears I cried. I couldn't breathe out of my nose because it was so stuffy from crying. While lying on the bathroom floor, I told myself that my kids would be better off without me. Their dad and his parents would take far better care of them than I was mentally and physically capable of.

All I wanted was to close my eyes, take one last breath and be done with this shit show of a life I created for myself. Thought after thought plagued my mind.

I should have purchased a house big enough for me to take care of my mom. I'm the worst daughter ever.

If my dad was still here everything would be ok.

My ex blames me for the demise of our marriage even though I knew all the blame wasn't on me. But I was the villain to him and everyone who would listen to his side of the story. I had a scarlet letter on my chest.

I was unlovable, a waste of space.

I couldn't give a kidney to my sister and felt guilty.

I laid on the floor and remembered what my mom used to say: "When you pray to God, just talk to Him like you would talk to me." That's what I did. I prayed like I've never prayed before. It was a different prayer from all the others. It felt like my soul was detached from my body and I was communing with God in a way like never before. I begged Him to take this darkness from my soul and to send help. In the midst of my storm, I could hear that still quiet voice: "Have faith the size of a mustard seed." I made one last attempt at saving myself. I called my ex from my bathroom floor. My tone and what I was saying was enough for him to leave his house at 2:00 am and literally save my life. Thankfully, in my moment of weakness, he still cared enough about me, and his kids, to not let me do anything to myself.

The next day, while at his house, I immediately called my therapist and told her what had happened. She asked some questions to ensure I wasn't still in a suicidal state and I wasn't. Oddly enough, I felt relieved talking to her. She gave me a number to a nurse practitioner (NP) at a psychiatrist's office, extra appointments with her twice a week and some homework to do daily to keep me sane until my appointment with the NP. The purpose of the NP was for her to do an assessment and prescribe medication. I was already on an antidepressant that was prescribed by a different NP at the Wellness Clinic at work but obviously, I needed something stronger. After about three months of being on the waitlist to see the NP, I finally found myself sitting on "The Couch." I would have never thought I would ever end up on "The Couch" in a psychiatrist's office. She changed my depression medication and added in a pill for my anxiety. Within 48 hours of starting my new cocktail, I felt like a brand new woman. I've never in my entire life felt so at peace and happy. It was at that moment I realized I had a chemical imbalance in my brain.

I've been on depression and anxiety medication for over a year now and it is literally the best thing I could have done for myself and my family. In the black and brown communities, there is a stigma that exists around mental health issues, taking prescribed psychotropic and seeking help from a licensed mental health provider. This invisible, but oh so real, stigma has not only taken away years of me being able to fully live life authentically, but has taken the lives of so many beautiful souls in our communities. Historically, the black and brown communities are marginalized people in general due to the lack of resources for mental health, disparities in our economic status, and in the center of it all is racism. We must continue to advocate for mental health equality but be vulnerable in telling our stories and personal struggles.

I was afraid of being vulnerable but there is power in vulnerability. Vulnerability is a sign of strength and it allows you to reclaim your power. Vulnerability is a superpower and only few possess this power. This superpower can literally save lives if we all knew how to activate it. We cannot fully rely on governmental systems and structures to adequately provide mental health care to our communities. It takes a gang of superheroes with the power of vulnerability to break through the concrete walls of mental health layer by layer. It's time to activate your superpower with one simple first step and that's to have faith the size of a mustard seed. Plant that one seed of faith deep down in your soul and water it with self-love, compassion, grace, and gratitude. Love yourself enough to know that you are worthy of wholeness, mentally and physically. Give yourself compassion and accept where you are in the present moment. Add some grace in there and forgive yourself for past failures or mistakes. Lastly, live life daily with the spirit of gratitude. Give thanks for all blessings big and small. I wake up every morning with self-love, compassion, grace, and gratitude in my cup. When my cup is overflowing, I pour into others. That is how I activate my superpower. I challenge you to plant that seed of faith today. Keep that seed watered every day the best you know how and go out in the world and help save the life of the next person who may be ready to end their own.

The Power of Vulnerability

You never know whose life you may save with one selfless act of pouring into someone else's cup.

Tiffany Winfield is a single mom of two, full-time Risk Specialist for Capital One and professionally trained Life Coach. Born and raised in the small southern town of Danville, VA, she left at the age of 17 to pursue her degree in Marketing at Virginia Commonwealth University (VCU) in Richmond, VA. In addition to obtaining her B.S. in Marketing, Tiffany also has a Master's Degree in Business Administration from Strayer University. When she is not working her full-time job, Tiffany dedicates a lot of her time loving on her kids, enjoying football games with her son, and developing her knowledge of mental health issues and the stigma it has on the black and brown communities.

Tiffany has developed a passion for encouraging and motivating individuals living with mental health issues; specifically, depression and anxiety. Living with depression, anxiety and PTSD herself, she understands the challenges that mental health issues present, even just performing basic day to day tasks. She has also found her purpose of empowering women to discover personal and professional freedom through strength, courage, faith, and self-awareness.

Tiffany Winfield

Tiffany has chosen to share her mental health journey and empower women through social media, her podcast Therapy, Wine and Jesus, Life Coaching, motivational speaking and other avenues to inspire and encourage other black and brown people to be vulnerable and share their stories as well. Doing so, she believes will end the stigma of mental health issues and create a path forward for better access to mental healthcare and break down the walls that prevent others suffering with mental health issues from living their best life!

Conclusion

Congratulations! You made it to the end of this book which means the stories of these women resonated with you in some way. As you read their stories, you could either empathize or relate to them or both. Whichever the case, we hope you no longer feel ashamed of the pain attached to your depression and anxiety. We hope the guilt has been erased from your heart and the shame has been swiped from your mind. You can now remove the mask that you've been hiding behind. You can now be seen and heard. You deserve to live a life of abundance. You deserve to live a life that is free. Go forth and #begreat.

www.ingramcontent.com/pod-product-compliance
Lightning Source LLC
Chambersburg PA
CBHW050705160426
43194CB00010B/2004